STANDARDS-BASED
CLASS BOOKS

30 Seasonal Book Activities for Emergent Writers

Written by
Traci Ferguson Geiser, MA

Editor: Heather Butler
Illustrator: Darcy Tom
Designer: Barbara Peterson
Cover Designer: Barbara Peterson
Art Director: Moonhee Pak
Project Director: Betsy Morris

Table of Contents

Introduction

Young children love to see their own work being published. *Standards-Based Class Books* features 30 fun-filled book-writing projects for the early childhood classroom. The collaborative books in this resource were designed to align with national language arts standards and cover several popular seasonal themes throughout the school year. There are ten books for each of the three seasons of the school year (September to June). As children contribute to each book and go through the publishing process, they will develop confidence as both writers and readers, and learn respect for classmates. These books that children have created themselves, the ones they have authored and illustrated, will surely become the most sought after, high-mileage books in the class-room. They are sure to be read again and again!

How to Use This Book

Each activity includes an objective, the language arts standards taught, a materials list, and a reproducible book page to quickly get you started. Review each activity beforehand, gather the materials, and complete any work that can be done in advance.

Standards Chart

If you have a specific lesson objective, refer to the language arts standards chart on pages 8 and 9 to help plan your lessons. This handy reference correlates national language arts standards to each class book.

Teaching Aids

In the Teaching Aids section of this book, you will find reproducible pages to help children with the book-writing process. For instance, the *Colors* teaching aid (page 93) reminds children of how to spell the names of colors. The *Numbers* teaching aid (page 94) shows the numeral, the number word, and the corresponding number of dots. The

Letters teaching aid (page 95) provides the correct formation of upper- and lowercase letters. Each of these pages is a helpful reference for children year-round and could be laminated and kept in their work area. This section also includes a Family Introduction Letter (page 96) to send home to introduce families to the collaborative book-writing process.

Literature Links

Refer to the Literature Links page located at the beginning of each seasonal section to find a suggested literature selection for each activity. These literature links will enrich your class's writing experience by providing models of good writing. They will help expand children's background knowledge so that they have more writing ideas and a better understanding of how to develop the ideas into a story.

Taking Dictation

As you and your class complete the activities in this resource, encourage children to write as much as they are developmentally able. Many young children will need to dictate to an adult. Taking dictation is a valuable method of support-ing children as writers, because it enables them to focus on the message they want to convey, and it fosters verbal fluency. When taking dictation, write down children's exact words and use appropriate capital letters and punctuation. Then ask children to "read" back the written words. As children's knowledge of writing progresses, their confidence will grow and the need for taking dictation will diminish.

School-to-Home Connection

The collaborative books described in this resource are great tools to strengthen the school-to-home connection. For some books, you may wish to begin the activities in the classroom and then send the book pages home with children so that they can finish them with their parents.

My favorite winter celebration is Chinese New Year because...

Ideas for Publishing

Book Covers—Add a card stock cover to each book. Be sure to include the title, authors (e.g., *Miss Butler's Class*), and the date of publication. Either invite children to help decorate it in class or send it home as a family project.

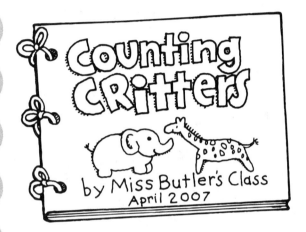

About the Authors—In the back of the book, include a class picture. Have each child dictate a sentence about himself or herself.

Book Binding Ideas

Each of the following bindings will allow you to take the books apart so that each child can take his or her pages home at the end of the year:

• **Loose-Leaf Rings**—These rings come apart easily for the teacher, but little ones can't get them open. Hole-punch the pages, and clip them together with a few rings. These work great if you would like to hang your books on the wall to display them! Ring-Its™ (CTP 1748) are available online at www.creativeteaching.com or in teacher

stores for the purpose of binding books such as the ones described in this resource.

• **Comb Bindings**—If your school has a binding machine, this is a great way to bind your class books. This process can also be done at most copy stores for a fee. Also, at the end of the year this sturdy binding can easily be taken apart using the binding machine. Each child's pages can be collated together and rebound with a binding comb. If you choose not to rebind the books, you may want to make enough books so that every child in the class can take a different book home at the end of the year.

• **Presentation Binders**—These handy fold-ers are bound with page protectors already inside of them. Simply slip two book pages in back-to-back and your book is ready to be read! These folders are less bulky than three-ring binders and fit easily inside a book rack in a classroom library.

• **Three Ring Binders**—Three-hole punch each page, and put it into a three-ring binder. Use one with a clear pocket cover that will allow you to slip a cover page in the front. Putting the pages inside page protectors will keep them neat.

• **Yarn**—Want a simple, inexpensive, and readily available binding? Use yarn. Hole punch the pages, tie them together with yarn or a pretty ribbon, and you have a book. These are great if children are making their own books in the writing center. This binding works best on laminat-ed pages. You can also add reinforcements over the holes in the punched pages to prevent tearing.

Enjoying the Books

Classroom Library—After each book is complete, read it together as a class. Children will take great pride in sharing their work. Also, invite children to explain their page to the class. Keep the books in the class library or other easily accessible location for children to read at their leisure. They will enjoy looking at books they have created with their class, a great motivator to get them into print!

Sharing Books with Families—Children will enjoy sharing their class books with their family! Children will become avid readers and gain valuable practice as they share these books with family and friends. Attach a class list to the back cover of each book. Place the books into resealable plastic bags. Allow children to take the books home and read them with their family. After they have read the book, have them place a check mark next to their name. Continue to rotate each book until everyone in the class has had a turn to take it home. You may have several books rotating at a time and the other books remaining in the classroom library for children to enjoy at school.

Taking Books Home at the End of the Year—Near the end of school, gather all of the class books written during the school year. Set aside time for each child to take a turn reading a class book to the class, or ask parent volunteers to help read aloud the books. Decide if you would like each child to take home a different class book or take home his or her own pages. Either have a drawing in which each of the books will be given to a different child to take home or disassemble each book and bind each child's pages together to create a treasury for each child to take home and enjoy for years.

Language Arts Standards Chart

FALL	ABC Name Book	Birthday Bash	School Is Cool!	Count on My Family	Colorful Apples	Fall Leaf Rhyme Time	Pick a Pumpkin	Itsy Bitsy Spider	Create a Costume	Thankful Turkeys
MECHANICAL CONVENTIONS										
Use conventions of capitalization	●									
Use conventions of punctuation		●								
Use conventions of print										
GRAMMATICAL CONVENTIONS										
Use nouns										
Use adjectives		●					●			
Use verbs										
READING SKILLS AND STRATEGIES										
Know some letters of the alphabet	●									
Distinguish between letters and numbers										
Decode unknown words										
Use phonics to spell simple words										●
Know that print appears in different forms										
VOCABULARY										
Understand sight words and vocabulary					●					●
Use new vocabulary to describe										
COMPREHENSION										
Sequence events in a story								●		
Relate information to prior knowledge										
Summarize information									●	
Differentiate between real and make-believe										
LISTENING AND SPEAKING										
Dictate stories, poems, and personal narratives										
Tell stories								●		
Use descriptive words to convey ideas							●			
Use interrogative sentences										
Contribute in class and group discussions										
WRITING PROCESS										
Write familiar words			●	●	●					
Write for a variety of purposes									●	
Use prewriting strategies			●							
Use strategies to organize written work										
Use writing to describe familiar things					●					
Write in a variety of forms or genres										
AUDITORY DISCRIMINATION										
Know that syllables make up words										
Identify rhymes and rhyming sounds						●				
Discriminate the sounds of spoken language						●				

	WINTER										SPRING									
	Super Soup	Headed South	Falling Snow	Winter Wear	Winter ABC Book	Celebrations	Snow Play	Building a Snowman	Question for the President	Be My Valentine	Springtime Syllables	Springtime Trees	Dr. Seuss's Make-Believe World	March Money	Growing Gardens	Counting Critters	Farm Animals	Marvelous Mommies	Farewell Friends	Super Dads
									•											
				•											•		•			
																•	•			•
																		•		
					•															
																•				
											•									
														•						
	•																		•	
		•											•							
							•					•								
													•							
			•															•		
		•																		
									•											
						•														
				•											•					
	•													•						
								•												
								•												
			•		•	•						•								•
										•									•	
											•									
				•																

9

Fall Literature Links

ABC Name Book
A, My Name Is Alice
by Jane E. Bayer (DIAL BOOKS)

Birthday Bash
A Birthday for Frances
by Russell Hoban (HARPERCOLLINS)

School Is Cool!
Clifford's First School Day
by Norman Bridwell (SCHOLASTIC)

Count on My Family
The Family Book
by Todd Parr (MEGAN TINGLEY BOOKS)

Colorful Apples
The Apple Pie Tree
by Zoe Hall (THE BLUE SKY PRESS)

Fall Leaf Rhyme Time
Red Leaf, Yellow Leaf
by Lois Ehlert (HARCOURT)

Pick a Pumpkin
Big Pumpkin
by Erica Silverman (SIMON & SCHUSTER)

Itsy Bitsy Spider
The Very Busy Spider
by Eric Carle (PHILOMEL)

Create a Costume
The Little Old Lady Who Was Not Afraid of Anything
by Linda Williams (HARPERCOLLINS)

Thankful Turkeys
Alligator Arrived with Apples
by Crescent Dragonwagon
(ATHENEUM BOOKS)

ABC Name Book

Children will identify the first letter of their name and create a page that includes a self portrait.

Materials

- *ABC Name Book* reproducible (page 12)
- index cards
- crayons or markers

Class Book Directions

1 In advance, copy a class set of the *ABC Name Book* reproducible. You will need to make an additional copy for each letter of the alphabet that is not represented by the first letter in children's names. Write each child's name on a separate index card.

2 Give children their name card and a copy of the book page. Have children write the first letter of their name capitalized in the box at the top of the page, using their name card as an aid if needed. Ask children to complete the sentence at the bottom of the page by writing their name in the first blank and the first letter of their name in the second blank.

3 Ask children to draw a self-portrait to complete their page. For younger children, draw the outline of an oval face to get them started.

4 For each letter not represented, ask children to brainstorm names of children in other classes or names of animals. Have children help complete those pages.

5 After all the pages are complete, have the class help arrange the pages in alphabetical order.

begins with

_____ begins with

Birthday Bash

Children will write or copy the month and day of their birthday. They will then complete a sentence to indicate what they do on their birthday.

Materials

- *Birthday Bash* reproducible (page 14)
- *Birthday Information* reproducible (page 15)
- craft sticks
- birthday wrapping paper
- scissors
- tape

Teaching the Standards

- Use adjectives in written compositions
- Use conventions of punctuation (exclamation points)

Class Book Directions

1 In advance, copy class sets of the *Birthday Bash* and *Birthday Information* reproducibles. Fill out a copy of the *Birthday Information* reproducible for each child. Draw an exclamation point on a separate craft stick for each child.

2 Explain to children that exclamation points are used in print when something exciting happens.

3 Give each child a craft-stick exclamation point. Ask children to think about the favorite part of their birthday. As children share their ideas, have them hold up their exclamation point and practice what they are saying with excitement.

4 Hand out a copy of the book page and their *Birthday Information* reproducible to each child. Show children where the month and day of their birthday will be copied onto the book page. Demonstrate how to choose a favorite birthday activity and where to write it on the page. Ask children to dictate or write in their birthday activity in the blanks.

5 Invite children to draw a picture in the box of themselves on their birthday doing the activity they wrote about. Cut wrapping paper into 5-inch (13 cm) squares and place a wrapping paper square over each picture. Tape the top edge to the page to make a flap. Children can peek inside the box on each page as they enjoy the book.

My birthday is on _____.

name

I love to _____ on my birthday!

Standards-Based Class Books © 2007 Creative Teaching Press

Birthday Information

Name: _____

My birthday is on:

January	1	17
February	2	18
March	3	19
April	4	20
May	5	21
June	6	22
July	7	23
August	8	24
September	9	25
October	10	26
November	11	27
December	12	28
	13	29
	14	30
	15	31
	16	

I love to _____ on my birthday!

open gifts

play games

eat cake

have a party

be with my family

go out to eat

School Is Cool!

Children will write what they like best about school and illustrate it to complete their book page.

Teaching the Standards

- Use prewriting strategies to plan written work (discuss ideas)
- Use knowledge of letters to write or copy familiar words

Materials

- *School Is Cool!* reproducible (page 17)
- sentence strips
- pocket chart
- crayons or markers
- chart paper

Class Book Directions

1 In advance, copy a class set of the *School Is Cool!* reproducible. Write each child's name on a separate sentence strip.

2 Write the title *What We Like to Do at School* on a sentence strip. Place the title at the top of the pocket chart. Read it aloud and ask children what their favorite thing to do at school is. Write each child's answer on the back side of the sentence strip that has his or her name on it, and place the strips in the pocket chart with the answers showing.

3 Show children a copy of the book page, and read the rhyme to them. Demonstrate where they will write their name and what they like about school.

4 Hand out a copy of the book page to each child. Ask children to complete the sentence at the bottom of the page. Have the *What We Like to Do at School* chart available so that children can pick up their sentence strip and copy their answer if needed.

5 To complete their page, ask children to draw a picture of what they like to do at school.

6 As a math extension, make a class graph on chart paper to display in the classroom to show what children like best about school.

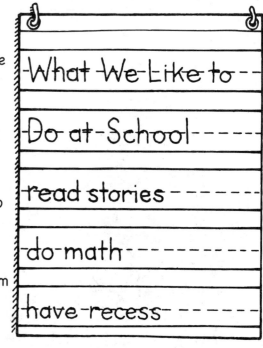

What We Like to
Do at School
read stories
do math
have recess

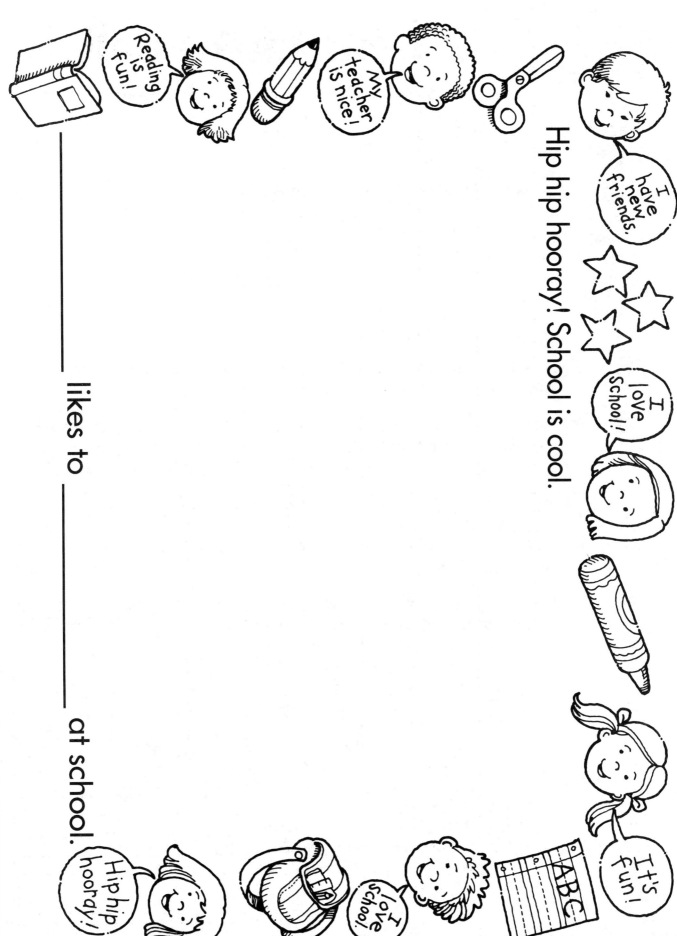

_____ likes to _____ at school.

Hip hip hooray! School is cool.

Count on My Family

Children will write number words to complete a page about the number of people in their family.

Teaching the Standards

- Use knowledge of letters to write or copy familiar words
- Use writing to describe familiar persons

Materials

- *The Family Book* by Todd Parr (MEGAN TINGLEY BOOKS)
- *Count on My Family* reproducible (page 19)
- *Numbers* teaching aid (page 94)
- chart paper
- crayons or markers

Class Book Directions

1. Copy a class set of the *Count on My Family* reproducible and the *Numbers* teaching aid.

2. Read aloud *The Family Book*. Discuss with children the different family members and types of families in the book. Invite children to make connections to their own family.

3. Ask each child to identify how many people are in his or her family. Record children's different answers in numerical order on chart paper (listing each number only once). Next to each number write the corresponding number word and number of dots.

4. Give each child a copy of the book page and *Numbers* teaching aid. Show children how to find the appropriate number word by identifying the correct number or counting the dots next to the word.

5. Ask children to write the correct number word on the line at the bottom of the page, using the *Numbers* teaching aid if needed.

6. Invite children to draw a portrait of their family in the frame of their book page. Help them write their family's name at the bottom of the frame.

Some families are big. Some families are small.

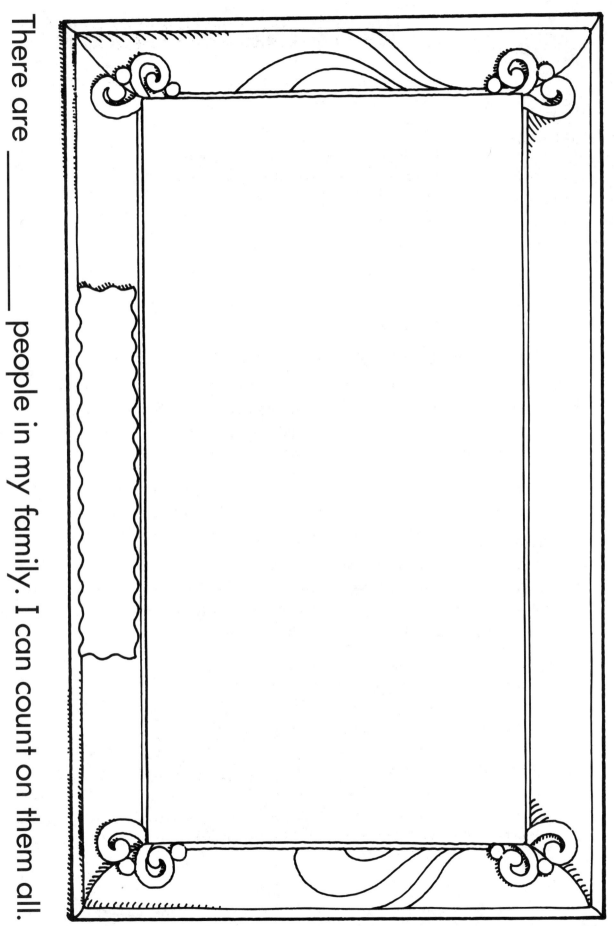

There are _____ people in my family. I can count on them all.

Colorful Apples

Children will taste red, green, and yellow apples and pick which color they prefer to eat. They will write which is their favorite color apple and why they like it.

Materials

- *Colorful Apples* reproducible (page 21)
- red, green, and yellow apples
- kitchen knife (teacher use only)
- plastic forks
- red, green, and yellow paint
- shallow paint trays
- chart paper
- red, green, and yellow markers and colored pencils

Class Book Directions

1. Copy a class set of the *Colorful Apples* reproducible. Cut several apples of different colors in half from top to bottom and insert a fork in the back of each. Cut the remainder of the apples into slices. Pour a small amount of red, green, and yellow paint into separate paint trays.

2. Show children the different colors of apples. Have them name each color. Use the correctly colored marker to write each of the color words on chart paper.

3. Invite children to taste a slice of each color of apple. Ask each child to take a colored pencil in the color of the apple he or she likes best. Give each child a copy of the book page. Have children use the colored pencil to write in the color word for their favorite apple in the first blank on the crayon. On the second blank, have children write or dictate what they like about the apple they chose.

4. Have children choose an apple half of the color they wrote about. Holding it by the fork, children should first dip the flat part of the apple in the matching color of paint, and then press the apple on their book page to make a print. Set the pages aside to dry and then assemble the book.

Red, yellow, and green apples—they're all good for me.

If I had to choose one, this is what it would be:

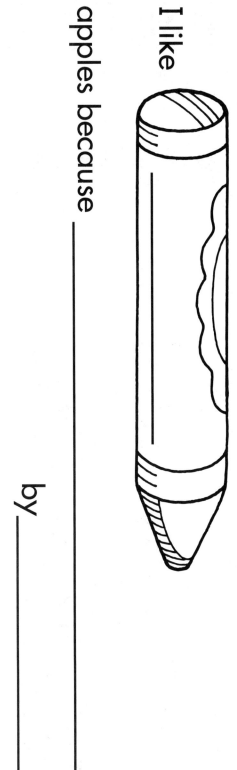

I like

apples because _____

_____.

by _____

Fall Leaf Rhyme Time

Children will finish a rhyme from a choice of words and make a leaf rubbing to complete their page.

Materials

• *Fall Leaf Rhyme Time* reproducible (page 23)
• *Fall Rhyme Cards* (page 24)
• tape
• assorted artificial leaves with prominent veins

• sentence strips
• pocket chart
• chart paper
• markers
• fall-colored crayons with paper labels removed

Class Book Directions

1. Copy a class set of the *Fall Leaf Rhyme Time* reproducible. Copy and cut apart several sets of the *Fall Rhyme Cards* so that each child has a variety from which to choose. Tape leaves to a table with the vein side up. Copy the rhyme from the book page onto sentence strips, and place them in a pocket chart.

2. Show children the rhyme in the pocket chart. Read aloud the rhyme several times, each time inserting a different fall rhyme card into the blank as you read.

3. Have children choose a rhyme card for their page of the book, and give them a copy of the book page. Show children where to copy the word from their card to complete the rhyme.

4. Give children markers to draw a large illustration of their rhyming word on the bottom half of their book page. Have each child choose a crayon to make a leaf rubbing. Help children position their drawing over the leaf so the rubbing looks like the leaf is falling on the object. (You may want to have children practice rubbings on scratch paper first.)

5. Assemble the book and place it in a reading corner for children to enjoy.

Fall leaves are everywhere,

Fall leaves fell on the _____.

by _____

Fall Rhyme Cards

stairs

bear

pear

hair

square

chair

Pick a Pumpkin

Children will select from a choice of adjectives and finger-paint an illustration to complete their book page.

Teaching the Standards

- Use descriptive words to convey basic ideas
- Use adjectives in written compositions

Materials

- *Pick a Pumpkin* reproducible (page 26)
- *Pumpkin Cards* (pages 27–28)
- pumpkins of various sizes, textures, and shapes
- orange fingerpaint
- finger-painting paper
- crumpled paper
- bubble wrap

Class Book Directions

1. Make a copy of the *Pick a Pumpkin* reproducible for each child. Make enough copies of the *Pumpkin Cards* so that each child has a variety from which to choose.

2. Set out several pumpkins for children to examine and feel. Discuss with them how each one is different.

3. Read aloud the word on the bottom of each pumpkin card and discuss with children what each word means. Invite children to take turns matching the appropriate card to the pumpkins.

4. Read to the class the rhyme on the bottom of the book page. Ask each child to decide which pumpkin he or she would choose from the pumpkin patch and to select the appropriate card.

5. Have children sit in a circle holding their card. Walk around the center of the circle saying the book page's rhyme. When you come to the blank, choose a child to come to the center of the circle and say the word on his or her card to fill in the blank. Have that child repeat the poem. Continue this activity until all children have had a turn.

6. Give each child a book page. Have children copy the word from their card to fill in the blank.

7. Invite children to finger-paint a picture of their type of pumpkin on finger-painting paper to add to their book page. Provide crumpled paper and bubble wrap for children to add texture to their painted pumpkin.

Pumpkins, pumpkins, mix or match.

I'll pick a _____ pumpkin from the patch.

by _____

Pumpkin Cards

big

small

round

bumpy

Pumpkin Cards

skinny

fat

tall

short

Standards-Based Class Books © 2007 Creative Teaching Press

Itsy Bitsy Spider

Children will sequence the events in their own version of "The Itsy Bitsy Spider" and share their story with the class.

Materials

- *The Itsy Bitsy Spider* reproducible (page 30)
- black washable ink pad
- baby wipes
- black, thin-line markers

Teaching the Standards

- Know the sequence of events in a story
- Tell stories based on personal experience or make-believe

Class Book Directions

1. Copy a class set of *The Itsy Bitsy Spider* reproducible.

2. Tell children that they are going to make up their own story about the Itsy Bitsy Spider in which they get to decide what the spider climbs up and what makes him fall. Make up a story together to give children ideas to get them started.

3. Give each child a copy of the reproducible. In the box on the left, have children draw a picture of what object the spider climbed up (e.g., a tree, a rock, a person's leg) without drawing the spider. Have them write the number *one* on the line below the box. Ask children to think of something that might happen to the spider to make it fall. In the middle box, invite children to draw the same scene as the first, but add what made the spider fall (e.g., snow, a wave, a person's hand swatting at it). Have them write the number *two* on the line below this box. In the last box, have children draw the ending to the story and write the number *three* on the line below.

4. To complete their page, help children press their thumb on the ink pad and print it on each of their pictures to make their spider's body. After children are finished printing, hand out baby wipes for fast cleanup. Next, have children use a black, thin-line marker to draw in the eight legs on each spider.

The Itsy Bitsy Spider

by _____

Create a Costume

Children will create a list by writing or copying items they would need to complete a costume.

Materials

- *The Little Old Lady Who Was Not Afraid of Anything* by Linda Williams (HARPERCOLLINS)
- *Costume Shopping List* reproducible (page 32)
- *Costume List* reproducible (page 33)
- chart paper
- art paper

Class Book Directions

1. In advance, copy class sets of the *Costume Shopping List* and *Costume List* reproducibles. If needed, trim art paper to the same size as the book reproducible.

2. Read aloud *The Little Old Lady Who Was Not Afraid of Anything*. At the end of the story, ask children to help retell the story by naming all of the items that made up the scarecrow. Write this list on chart paper (i.e., a jack-o'-lantern mask, a shirt and pants with patches, boots, a hat, and gloves), and talk about how lists help us.

3. Ask children to name other fun characters to dress up as. On chart paper, record the items needed to complete the costumes.

4. Tell children that they are going to write a list of items needed for a costume they would like to wear.

5. Give each child a copy of the *Costume Shopping List* and *Costume List* reproducibles. Let children know that they may use items from the Costume List, the lists created together, or their own ideas. Ask children to write their list on their own book page (or have them dictate it to an adult).

6. Invite children to draw a picture of themselves in their costume on a piece of landscape-oriented art paper. Assemble the book so that the corresponding lists and pictures face each other.

Costume Shopping List

1. _____
2. _____
3. _____
4. _____
5. _____
6. _____
7. _____
8. _____

Costume List

hat

cape

fangs

wig

boots

shoes

pants

dress

jewelry

broom

makeup

bag

mask

wings

glasses

mustache

gloves

magic wand

clown nose

white sheet

Thankful Turkeys

Children will write three things for which they are thankful.

Materials

- *Thankful Turkeys* reproducible (page 35)
- *Letters* teaching aid (page 95)
- small feathers in assorted colors
- chart paper
- glue

Class Book Directions

1. Copy a class set of the *Thankful Turkeys* reproducible. Copy the *Letters* teaching aid, if needed.

2. Show children the different colors of feathers. Hold up feathers one at a time, and ask children to name the colors as you record the color names on chart paper.

3. Have a class discussion about what the word *thankful* means. Have children think of items for which they are thankful that are the same colors as the feathers (e.g., yellow corn, red apples). Invite children to help write the responses on chart paper. Point out that words are always written from left to right and lists go from the top of the page to the bottom.

4. Give each child a copy of the book page. Ask children to write their name on the line on the turkey's body. Challenge them to write one colorful thing they are thankful for on each line. They may use a copy of the *Letters* teaching aid if needed. Have children who are unable to write letters or don't know the letter sounds dictate the words to an adult.

5. Invite children to glue the three corresponding colors of turkey feathers on their turkey to finish their page.

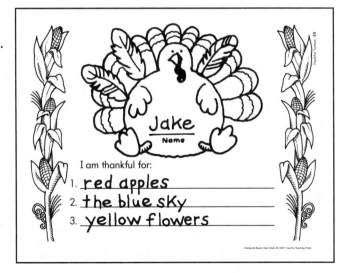

I am thankful for:

1. _____

2. _____

3. _____

Name

Winter Literature Links

Super Soup
Alvie Eats Soup
by Ross Collins (ARTHUR A. LEVINE BOOKS)

Headed South
Time to Sleep
by Denise Fleming (HENRY HOLT AND COMPANY)

Falling Snow
The Snowy Day
by Ezra Jack Keats (VIKING)

Winter Wear
Froggy Gets Dressed
by Jonathan London (VIKING)

Winter ABC Book
The Mitten
by Jan Brett (G. P. PUTNAM'S SONS)

Celebrations
Nine Spoons: A Chanukah Story
by Marci Stillerman (HACHAI PUBLISHING)

Snow Play
Katy and the Big Snow
by Virginia Lee Burton (HOUGHTON MIFFLIN)

Building a Snowman
The Biggest, Best Snowman
by Margery Cuyler (SCHOLASTIC)

Question for the President
What Presidents Are Made Of
by Hanoch Piven (ATHENEUM BOOKS)

Be My Valentine
The Valentine Bears
by Eve Bunting (CLARION)

Super Soup

Children will create a can label for their own unique flavor of soup.

Materials

- *Super Soup* reproducible (page 38)
- resealable sandwich bags
- assorted soup cans
- crayons or markers

- large pot
- soup ladle
- bowls
- plastic spoons

Class Book Directions

1. In advance, send each child home with a resealable sandwich bag requesting it to be returned with his or her favorite bite-sized snack (e.g., goldfish crackers) inside. Copy a class set of the *Super Soup* reproducible.

2. Pass around soup cans and point out the pictures and words on the labels. Tell children that they are going to create a soup label for their own special kind of soup. Ask children to give some ideas of the soup they would like to eat. Encourage children to be creative and come up with soups that they would not find at the grocery store (e.g., chocolate soup or jelly bean soup).

3. Give each child a copy of the book page. Show children how to write their name on the top line and the name of their soup on the bottom line. If they are unable to write it on their own, they can dictate it to an adult.

4. Invite children to finish their page by decorating their soup label and drawing a picture of their soup in the pot.

5. Make "class soup" by mixing together the snacks brought by the children. Invite children to help name the soup. Ladle the soup into bowls for children to snack on as each child shares his or her page with the class and tells what ingredients are in his or her soup.

I made some soup.

I made it hot.

I think I'll make another pot.

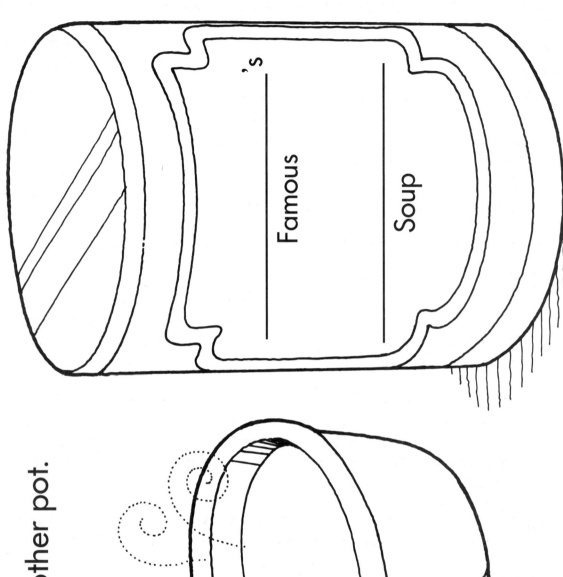

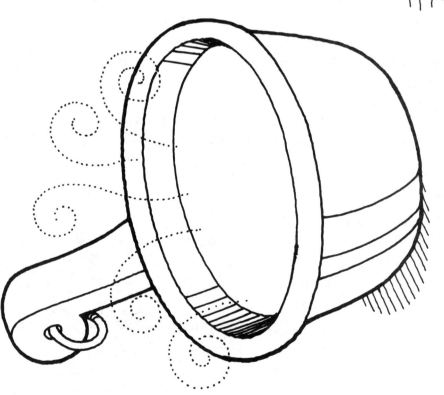

's

Famous

Soup

Headed South

Children will write about a place they would like to go when it gets cold in the winter.

Teaching the Standards

- Use new vocabulary to describe feelings, thoughts, experiences, and observations
- Tell stories based on personal experience or make-believe

Materials

- *Headed South* reproducible (page 40)
- globe
- flashlight
- pictures of warm weather locations
- paint, assorted colors
- feathers
- paintbrushes

Class Book Directions

1. Make a class set of the *Headed South* reproducible.

2. Ask children where they go or what they do when it gets cold. Have several children share their ideas with the class. Have a class discussion about how animals take care of themselves when it is cold in the winter. Explain that some animals grow extra fur, some go to sleep in caves or burrows, and some migrate to a warmer place in the winter.

3. Show children a globe and tell them that this is what Earth looks like from far away. Shine a flashlight on the globe to show how the sun warms the Earth. Show children the pictures of places that animals could migrate to. Point out these places on the globe. Hang up these pictures and label them with their names.

4. Give each child a copy of the reproducible. Ask children to choose from the pictures which place they would want to go to stay warm, and write it on their page. If needed, they can dictate it to an adult.

5. Tell children they will complete their page by painting a picture of themselves in the warm place they chose. Remind children that many birds fly to warm places, and invite them to paint the background of their picture with a feather.

If I wanted to stay warm during wintertime,

I would migrate to _____ for the winter.

Standards-Based Class Books © 2007 Creative Teaching Press

Falling Snow

Children will complete a sentence and draw a picture to indicate where snow can fall.

Materials

- *The Snowy Day* by Ezra Jack Keats (VIKING)
- *Falling Snow* reproducible (page 42)
- blue and white copy paper
- scissors
- white paint
- Styrofoam egg cartons
- white bedsheet
- chart paper

Class Book Directions

1. In advance, copy on blue paper a class set of the *Falling Snow* reproducible. Cut white paper into several small snowflakes. Pour white paint into Styrofoam egg cartons.

2. Read aloud *The Snowy Day*. Drape a white bedsheet across different objects in the room. Tell children that snow covers everything it falls on.

3. Gather children in a circle and teach them the poem from the book page. Walk around the circle as they recite it and drop a paper snowflake on a child. Have children complete the poem by saying that child's name. Repeat this activity until each child has been named.

4. Title a piece of chart paper *Snow Is Falling*. Ask children to think of objects outside that snow might cover. Below the title, draw a quick sketch of the children's answers and label each object. Read the list together.

5. Give each child a copy of the *Falling Snow* reproducible. Show children where they will write the name of one of the objects from the list. Keep the chart paper visible so children can copy their word if needed.

6. After they have completed the sentence, ask children to draw a picture of the object they wrote about. Explain that they will be adding "snow" to complete their picture. Invite children to dip a fingertip in the white paint and touch it to their picture several times to add snow.

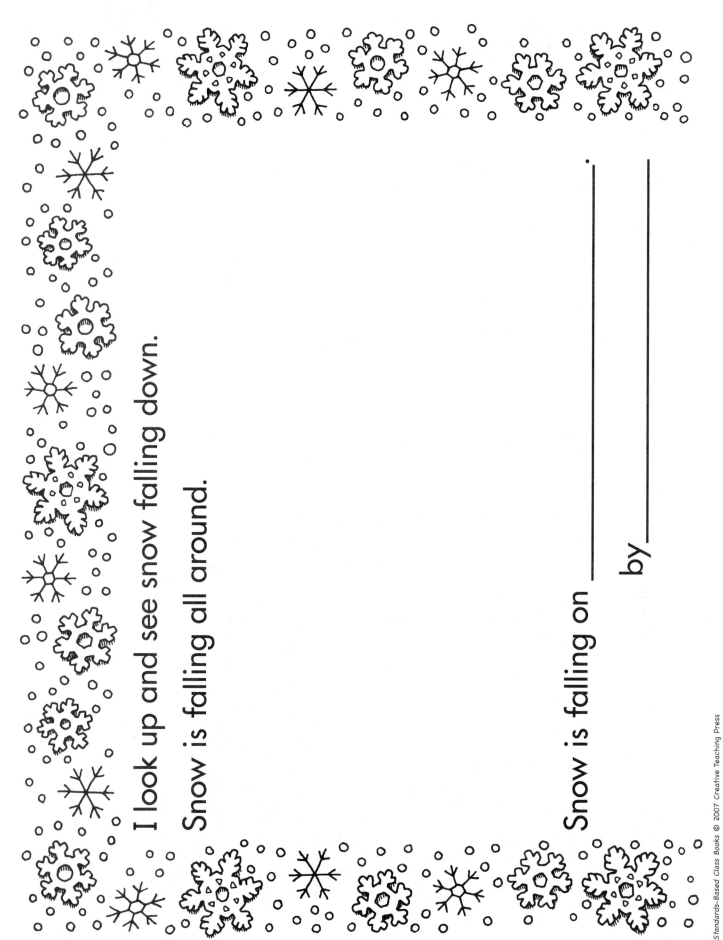

I look up and see snow falling down.

Snow is falling all around.

Snow is falling on _____.

by _____

Standards-Based Class Books © 2007 Creative Teaching Press

Winter Wear

Children will write about the winter clothing they would wear to stay warm and "dress" themselves to complete their page.

Materials

- *Froggy Gets Dressed* by Jonathan London (VIKING)
- *Winter Wear* reproducible (page 44)
- *Winter Wear Cards* (pages 45–46)
- winter clothing
- markers and crayons
- scissors
- glue

Class Book Directions

1 Copy a class set of the *Winter Wear* reproducible. Reproduce enough *Winter Wear Cards* so that each child can choose several.

2 Set out some winter clothing. Tell children that these clothing items help to keep you warm when the weather is cold.

3 Read aloud *Froggy Gets Dressed*. Have children list the different clothing that Froggy (or they) would put on to play in the snow. Set out the matching winter wear card as children name each item.

4 Give each child a copy of the *Winter Wear* reproducible. Tell children that they are going to pick the winter clothing they would wear to complete their page. Ask each child to choose a few winter wear cards.

5 Have children list the items they chose on their *Winter Wear* reproducible. Invite them to color and cut out their cards. Help children "dress" themselves by gluing their cutouts to the child on their book page, and have them add facial features to it to match their own.

6 Set out the completed book with the winter clothing. Invite children to dress up in the clothing as they enjoy the book.

When it's cold
and there's
a storm,

I must wear
winter clothes
to stay warm.

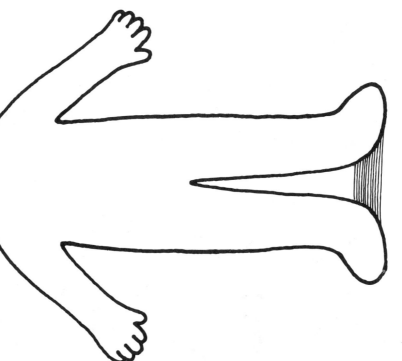

I would wear: _____

by _____

Standards-Based Class Books © 2007 Creative Teaching Press

Winter Wear Cards

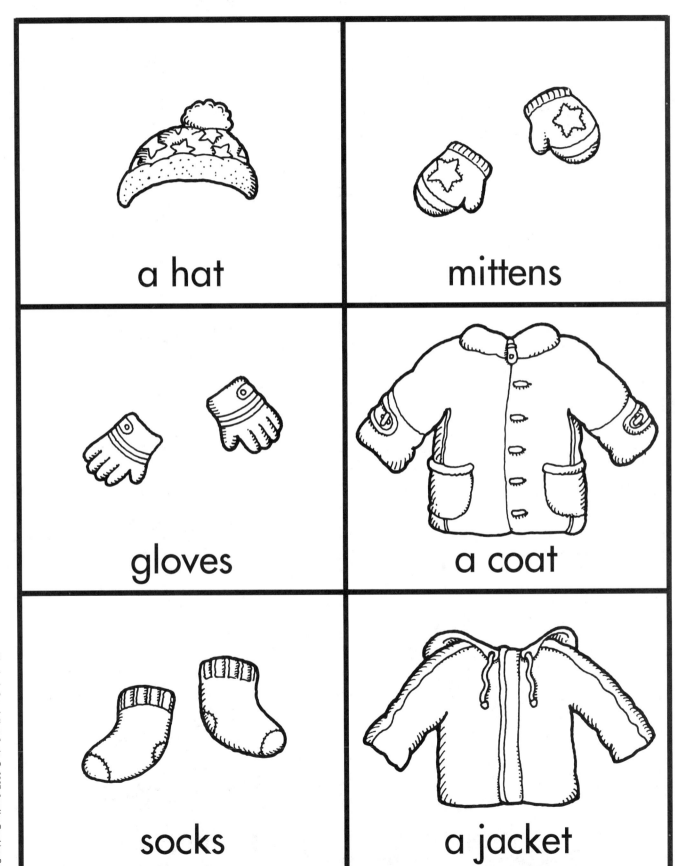

a hat

mittens

gloves

a coat

socks

a jacket

Winter Wear Cards

a scarf

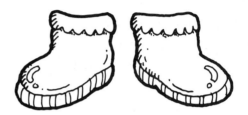

boots

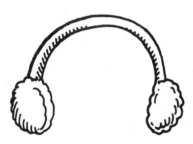

earmuffs

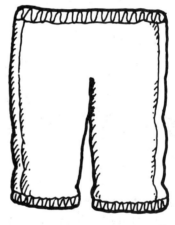

snow pants

long underwear

a sweater

Winter ABC Book

Children will identify the beginning letter of a winter-related word and finger-paint an illustration.

Teaching the Standards

- Know some letters of the alphabet
- Discriminate the sounds of spoken language

Materials

- *Winter ABC Book* reproducible (page 48)
- *Letters* teaching aid (page 95)
- *Winter Alphabet Ideas* (page 49)
- chart paper
- non-menthol shaving cream
- paper towels
- dry tempera paint

Class Book Directions

1 Make 26 copies of the *Winter ABC Book* reproducible. If children need help writing letters, make copies of the *Letters* teaching aid.

2 Write the letters A–Z vertically on a piece of chart paper. Ask children to help think of something about winter that begins with each letter. Write the words next to the letter they start with. Continue until each letter of the alphabet has a winter word (see *Winter Alphabet Ideas*, page 49).

3 Assign each child a different winter word from the list. If needed, challenge some children to make an additional page so that each letter of the alphabet is covered.

4 Gather children at tables. Squirt some shaving cream on the table in front of each child. Invite children to practice tracing their word in the make-believe snow (i.e., shaving cream). Use dry paper towels to clean up shaving cream.

5 Give each child a copy of the book page. Have children write their name in the first blank. Show children how to write the winter word on the next line and the beginning letter on the last line.

6 Squirt a small amount of shaving cream onto each book page. Sprinkle dry tempera paint onto the shaving cream. To complete the page, invite each child to finger-paint with the colorful shaving cream to make a snow painting of his or her word.

Winter words are in this book.

Here's _____'s page. Take a look!

_____ starts with _____

Winter Alphabet Ideas

Aa arctic fox, avalanche, angel, Antarctica

Bb bear, boots, blanket

Cc coat, cold, cocoa, Christmas

Dd drift, dreidel, dogsled, drum, deer

Ee eggnog, earmuffs

Ff fire, freeze, frost, flakes

Gg gloves, Groundhog Day

Hh hat, hot chocolate, hockey, hibernate, Hanukkah

Ii icicles, ice-skating, ice, igloo

Jj jacket, jingle bells

Kk Kwanzaa, kinara (Kwanzaa candle holder)

Ll long underwear, luge

Mm mittens, mistletoe, menorah, migrate

Nn (winter) naps, North Pole

Oo outside, Olympics

Pp popcorn, penguin, President's Day

Qq quilt

Rr runny nose, reindeer

Ss sled, scarf, snow, snowman, snowball, snowboard, ski

Tt toboggan, tissue, tubing

Uu umbrella

Vv valentines

Ww walrus, weather, Washington, wreath, winter wear

Xx extreme sports, extremely cold, ax (to cut firewood)

Yy Yule log

Zz Zamboni, zzzz (hibernating animals), zipper up

Celebrations

Children will write what their favorite winter celebration is and why, and draw a picture of themselves at the celebration.

Teaching the Standards

- Make contributions in class and group discussions
- Use writing to describe familiar persons, places, or experiences

Materials

- *Celebrations* reproducible (page 51)
- *Winter Celebrations* reproducible (page 52)
- crayons or markers
- craft supplies (e.g., tinsel, glitter, heart stickers, wrapping paper)
- glue

Class Book Directions

1. Copy class sets of the *Celebrations* and *Winter Celebrations* reproducibles. Have a group discussion about celebrations that occur in the winter (see *Winter Celebrations* reproducible, page 52). Ask children to share what they like best about the holidays they celebrate with their family.

2. Ask children to select their favorite winter celebration. Tell them to think about why it is their favorite and what they enjoy about it. Ask each child to share his or her favorite celebration with the class. If a child's answer is not included on the *Winter Celebrations* reproducible, write it on the back of the page for him or her to copy.

3. Give each child a copy of the book page and *Winter Celebrations* reproducible. Have children copy the name of their favorite celebration on the first line and then write why they like it or what they like about it on the following line. If children are unable to write or sound out their answer, have them dictate it to an adult.

4. To finish their page, ask children to draw a picture of themselves at their favorite winter celebration. Set out craft supplies for children to use in decorating their picture.

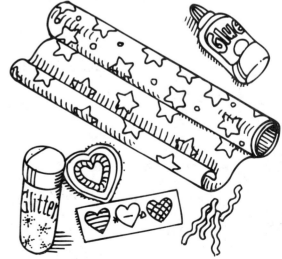

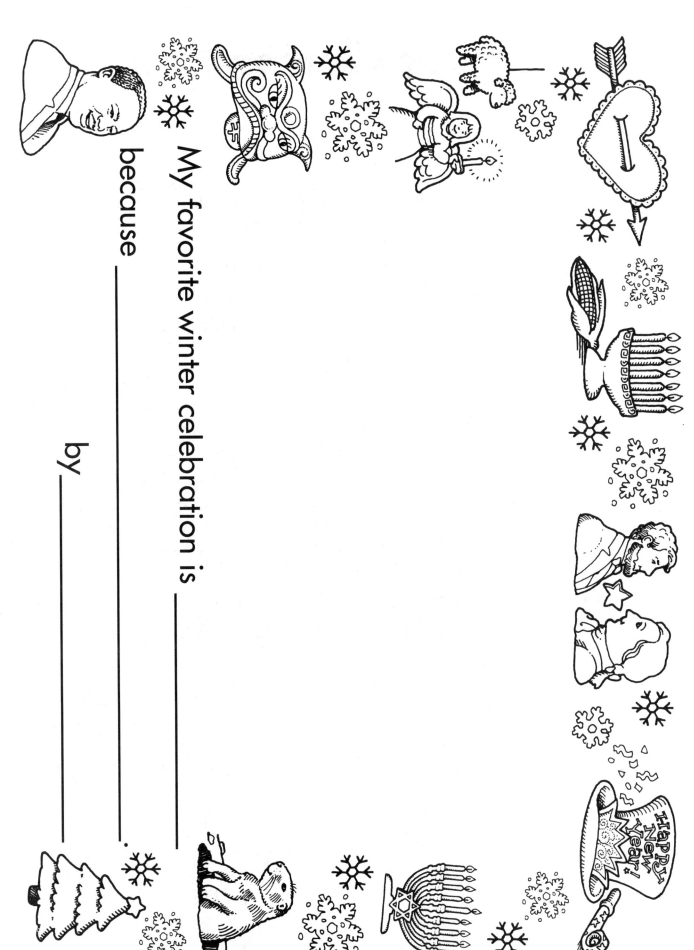

My favorite winter celebration is _____

because _____

_____.

by _____

Standards-Based Class Books © 2007 Creative Teaching Press

Winter Celebrations

Christmas

Las Posadas

Hanukkah

Kwanzaa

New Year's Day

Chinese New Year

Martin Luther King Jr. Day

Presidents' Day

Groundhog Day

Valentine's Day

Standards-Based Class Books © 2007 Creative Teaching Press

Snow Play

Children will complete the page by adding their favorite snow activity and drawing a picture of themselves doing it.

Materials

- *Snow Play* reproducible (page 54)
- *Winter Activity Cards* (pages 55–56)
- winter sports equipment
- mittens or gloves (one set per child)
- white paper towels

Teaching the Standards

- Use writing to describe familiar persons, places, or experiences
- Relate new information to prior knowledge and experiences

Class Book Directions

1 In advance, ask children, parents, and school staff members to bring in mittens or gloves and winter sports equipment or pictures. Invite adults to come in to share their winter experiences with the class. Crumple up a sufficient amount of white paper towels into "snowballs" for a "snowball fight."

2 Make a class set of the *Snow Play* reproducible. Copy and cut apart enough *Winter Activity Cards* so that each child can choose from a variety of cards.

3 Ask children which winter activities they have participated in and invite children to describe the different activities. If you live in a climate where it does not snow, you may want to find books at the library about various cold-weather sports and activities to show children.

4 Give each child a pair of mittens or gloves. Set out the paper-towel "snowballs" and invite children to participate in a pretend snowball fight.

5 Give each child a copy of the book page reproducible. Ask them to choose a winter activity card for the activity they would most like to do in the snow. Show them how to write their name on the first blank and the name of their favorite winter activity on the next blank.

6 Have children complete the page by drawing a picture of themselves participating in the winter activity.

make a snow angel

It's wintertime, this we know.

_____ likes to _____ when there is snow.

Winter Activity Cards

go sledding

ski

build a snowman

make a snow angel

have a snowball fight

take a sleigh ride

Winter Activity Cards

ice-skate

snowshoe

go tubing

snowboard

build a snow fort

play ice hockey

Building a Snowman

Children will sequence the steps of building a snowman and "build" a sponge-painted snowman.

Materials

- *Building a Snowman* reproducible (page 58)
- *Snowman Plan Cards* (page 59)
- *Snowman Stencil* reproducible (page 60)
- scissors
- card stock
- index cards
- blue construction paper
- small square sponges
- white paint in shallow paint trays
- markers

Class Book Directions

1. Make a class set of the *Building a Snowman* reproducible and *Snowman Plan Cards*. Cut apart and group each set of the cards. Make several copies on card stock of the *Snowman Stencil* reproducible. Cut along the lines of each snowman to make a stencil.

2. Discuss with children the process of building a snowman. Point out that some parts have to be done in a certain order or it will fall down.

3. Next, give each child a set of the *Snowman Plan Cards*. Divide the class into partners to discuss how they would like to complete their snowman. Help children put the cards in order.

4. Give children a copy of the book page. Show children how to take their first card and write that step on the first line of their book page. Have them continue until all steps are recorded, or invite them to dictate the text to an adult.

5. After children have completed their writing, give them a piece of blue construction paper and set out snowman stencils, sponges, and white paint. Help children sponge-paint a snowman (landscape-orientation on the paper) following the steps they recorded and using the stencil as a guide. Invite them to use markers to decorate their snowman.

Building a Snowman

1. _____
2. _____
3. _____
4. _____
5. _____
6. _____

by _____

Standards–Based Class Books © 2007 Creative Teaching Press

Snowman Plan Cards

Add arms.

Add a medium snowball.

Add a face.

Make a big snowball.

Add clothes.

Add a small snowball.

Snowman Stencil

Question for the President

Children will think of a question that they would like to ask the President to complete their page.

Materials

- *Question for the President* reproducible (page 62)
- blank index cards
- craft sticks
- tape
- 4" x 6" (10 x 15 cm) pieces of finger-painting paper
- red and blue finger paint

Class Book Directions

1. Copy a class set of the *Question for the President* reproducible. For each child, write a question mark on a separate index card. Tape each of these index cards to the top of a different craft stick.

2. Give each child a craft-stick question mark, and invite children to trace the question mark with their finger. Review what a question is and then alternately ask children a question or make a statement. Challenge children to hold up the question mark only after a question has been asked.

3. Discuss with them what the President's job is. Ask children what they think they might like to find out from the President.

4. Give each child a copy of the reproducible. Have them dictate their question for the President on their book page. Invite them to write the question mark at the end of the sentence.

5. To finish their page, invite children to draw a picture in the box of them meeting with the President. After the illustrations are finished, give each child a piece of finger-painting paper. Invite children to finger-paint a large red or blue question mark on the paper (landscape orientation). Tape the top part of each child's paper to the top of his or her picture to make a flap for children to lift up and see the illustrations as they enjoy the book. (Note: This book cannot have sheet protectors.)

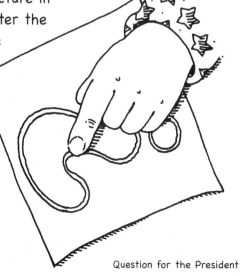

If I could ask the President one question, I would like to know:

by _____

Be My Valentine

Children will write the name of a classmate and make a valentine for that child to complete their page.

Materials

- *Be My Valentine* reproducible (page 64)
- glue
- 4 ⅜" x 5 ¾" (11 cm x 14.5 cm) envelopes
- index cards
- hat or other container
- coffee filters
- red, pink, and purple water-based markers
- scissors
- newspaper
- water spray bottle

Class Book Directions

1. Copy a class set of the *Be My Valentine* reproducible. Glue an envelope face-down in the center of each page. Write each child's name on a separate index card. Fold the cards in half and put them in a hat or other container.

2. Discuss with children what Valentine's Day is and why we give valentines. Tell children that valentines are given to friends to let them know they are special.

3. Tell children that they are going to make a book that contains a valentine for everyone in the class. Have each child draw a name from the hat and explain that they will make a page for that person.

4. Give each child a copy of the book page with an envelope attached. Show children how to write *to* and their friend's name on the outside of the envelope flap and then *from* and their own name on the inside of the flap.

5. Give each child a coffee filter. Invite children to color the coffee filters with red, pink, and purple water-based markers.

6. Challenge children to cut their filter into a heart-shaped valentine. Invite children to set their heart cutout on newspaper and use a spray bottle to slightly wet it.

7. Let the cutouts dry overnight, then help children place their valentine cutout inside the envelope on their page.

Dear friend of mine,

Will you be my valentine?

Spring Literature Links

Springtime Syllables
Hello Spring!
by Mary Packard (SCHOLASTIC)

Springtime Trees
When Spring Comes
by Robert Maass (HENRY HOLT AND COMPANY)

Dr. Seuss's Make-Believe World
Hop on Pop
by Dr. Seuss (RANDOM HOUSE)

March Money
St. Patrick's Day in the Morning
by Eve Bunting (CLARION BOOKS)

Growing Gardens
Growing Vegetable Soup
by Lois Ehlert (RED WAGON BOOKS)

Counting Critters
Going to the Zoo
by Tom Paxton (HARPERCOLLINS)

Farm Animals
Barnyard Banter
by Denise Fleming
(OWLET/HENRY HOLT AND COMPANY)

Marvelous Mommies
The Mother's Day Mice
by Eve Bunting (CLARION BOOKS)

Farewell Friends
The Jolly Postman
by Allan Ahlberg and Janet Ahlberg
(LITTLE, BROWN AND COMPANY)

Super Dads
What Mommies Do Best;
What Daddies Do Best
by Laura Numeroff (SIMON & SCHUSTER)

Springtime Syllables

Children will write two springtime-related words that have the same number of syllables and draw a picture of them to complete their book page.

Teaching the Standards

- Know that words are made up of syllables
- Use basic elements of structural analysis (syllables) to decode unknown words

Materials

- *Springtime Syllables* reproducible (page 67)
- *Numbers* teaching aid (page 94)
- chart paper

Class Book Directions

1 In advance, copy a class set of the *Springtime Syllables* reproducible. You may wish to white out the period and final *s* in *syllables*, and then add a period at the end to make copies for children who choose words with one syllable. Reproduce the *Numbers* teaching aid, if needed.

2 Ask children to help brainstorm a list of words that make them think of spring. Write this list on chart paper. As you write each word, ask children to clap (or hop like a bunny for springtime fun!) and count the number of syllables in the word. Group the words according to the number of syllables as you write the number next to the word.

3 Tell children they are going to make a spring book about syllables. To complete the book, each child will need to think of two spring words that have the same number of syllables. Ask children to think of examples to share with the class.

4 Give each child a copy of the book page and a *Numbers* teaching aid, if needed. Ask them to clap or "bunny hop" the syllables as they tell you which two words they would like to have on their page.

5 Show children how to write their two words on the first two lines and the numeral or number word on the third line.

6 Invite children to add a picture of their words to complete the page.

A-pril

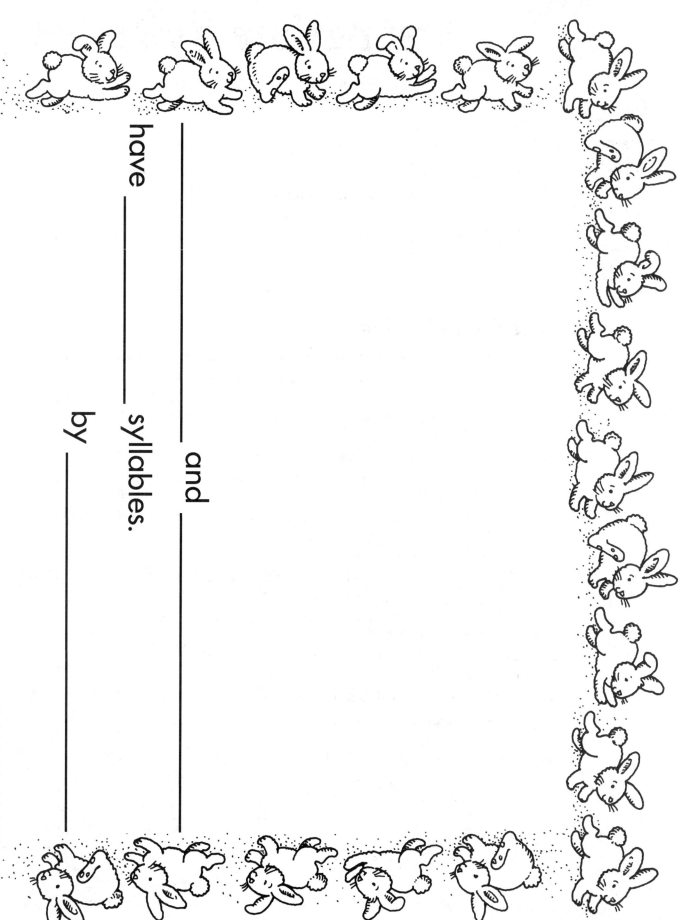

have _____ and _____ syllables.

by _____

Springtime Trees

Children will describe and paint a picture of the way trees look during the spring season.

Materials

- *Springtime Trees* reproducible (page 69)
- dandelions
- pictures of trees with blossoms and leaves
- sentence strips
- chart paper
- green, pink, and white paint
- shallow paint trays

Class Book Directions

1 In advance, copy a class set of the *Springtime Trees* reproducible. Collect several dandelions.

2 Set out a variety of pictures that have trees with blossoms, buds, or new leaves. Ask children to describe the different ways the trees look. Write each child's answer on a separate sentence strip.

3 Give each child a copy of the book page reproducible and the sentence strip with his or her answer on it, if needed. Invite children to copy the words from their sentence strip onto their book page.

4 Set out each color of paint in a separate paint tray and the dandelions. To finish their page, invite children to decorate their tree. To make leaves, show children how to dip a dandelion in the green paint and print it on the tree. To make blossoms, have children slightly dip a dandelion in either pink or white paint and print it on the tree. If children add both leaves and blossoms, have them add the leaves and let the paint dry before adding blossoms.

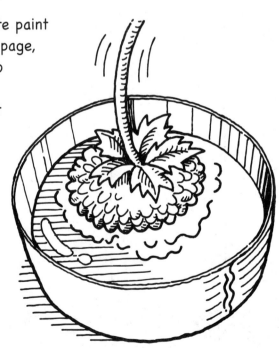

Trees in springtime
Change every day.
They look very different
From March to May!

I see _____

by _____ .

Dr. Seuss's Make-Believe World

Teaching the Standards

- Know the difference between fact and fiction, real and make-believe
- Use new vocabulary to describe feelings, thoughts, experiences, and observations

After listening to several Dr. Seuss books in honor of his birthday, March 2, children will create and describe a make-believe character to complete their page.

Materials

- *Volunteer Read-Aloud letter* (page 71)
- *Dr. Seuss's Make-Believe World* reproducible (page 72)
- Dr. Seuss books

Class Book Directions

1. In advance, copy the *Volunteer Read-Aloud letter*. Send a copy home with each child about a week before making the book. Copy a class set of the *Dr. Seuss's Make-Believe World* reproducible.

2. Talk with the class about the difference between real and make-believe. Discuss some characters in books that are real and some that are make-believe.

3. Invite volunteers and the children to dress up like their favorite Dr. Seuss character on the day that volunteers come to read aloud. Have volunteers rotate around the room and read aloud different Dr. Seuss books to small groups of children. Have each group talk about why the characters are make-believe (e.g., animals that talk or wear clothes would be make-believe because animals don't really do those things). Have them also discuss how they know when settings are make-believe.

4. Give each child a copy of the book page. Challenge children to draw a make-believe character on their book page. For instance, a child might draw a dog walking on its hind legs and carrying a purse.

5. Ask children to write why their character is make-believe.

Dear Family,

Please don't make a silly excuse.
Come and read us Dr. Seuss.
Having fun all the while—
Celebrating Dr. Seuss style!

We will be celebrating Dr. Seuss's birthday on March _____ from _____ to _____. In honor of Dr. Seuss Day, we will be making a class book to learn about real and make-believe.

Please sign and return this letter by _____. Thanks!

~~~~~~

❏ I plan to attend and read Dr. Seuss books to children.
❏ I will be unable to attend.

_____
parent/guardian

_____
phone

It could be big, it could be small,

But my character is not real at all.

It is make-believe because _____

_____. by _____

March Money

Children will write about and draw a picture of what they would like to buy if they found a leprechaun's pot of gold.

Materials

- *March Money* reproducible (page 74)
- crayons or markers

Teaching the Standards

- Use phonics knowledge to spell simple words
- Use emergent writing skills to write for a variety of purposes

Class Book Directions

1 Copy a class set of the *March Money* reproducible.

2 Lead a group discussion about St. Patrick's Day. Discuss the idea that sneaky little leprechauns cause mischief during this season. Tell children that legends say that leprechauns have a pot of gold at the end of the rainbow, and will give it to whomever can catch them.

3 Explain to children that gold is worth a lot of money. Ask children to think about what they would like to buy if they found a pot of gold.

4 Give each child a book page and read aloud the poem to the class. Explain that they will write in the blank what they would like to buy. Ask them to sound out each word as best they can. Don't worry about spelling. Instead, give each child the opportunity to write alone as much as he or she is developmentally able to. Give children the option of dictating it to an adult.

5 Once the writing is done, invite children to complete the page by adding a picture of the item they would like to purchase with their gold.

Leprechauns have gold we're told.

I'd buy _____

by _____ if I found their gold!

Growing Gardens

Children will choose a vegetable, copy its name, and make a pretend garden to complete their page.

Materials

- *Growing Vegetable Soup* by Lois Ehlert (RED WAGON BOOKS)
- *Growing Gardens* reproducible (page 76)
- *Veggie Cards* (pages 77–78)
- crayons or markers
- 4" x 6" (10 x 15 cm) pieces of sandpaper (one per child)
- glue

Class Book Directions

1 Copy a class set of the *Growing Gardens* reproducible. Copy and cut apart enough *Veggie Cards* so that each child can have a variety to choose from.

2 Read aloud *Growing Vegetable Soup*. Discuss which vegetables grew in that garden. Explain to children that they are going to make a book about a garden and that each child will need to pick a vegetable to include on his or her page.

3 Give each child a copy of the *Growing Gardens* reproducible. Have each child select a veggie card. Read aloud the rhyme on the book page, and show children where they will copy the name of their vegetable on the page.

4 After the writing is complete, invite children to color their veggie card. Then give each child a piece of sandpaper. Help children put glue along three sides of their sandpaper so that one of the longer sides does not have glue along it. Have them glue it to the center of their book page with the unglued side on top to create the "dirt" for their garden. Invite children to slide their veggie card under the top of their dirt to "plant" their vegetable. Invite children to draw more veggies across the top of their dirt and add a picture of themselves working in the garden.

5 While children look through the book, invite them to pull out the cards to "pick" the vegetables.

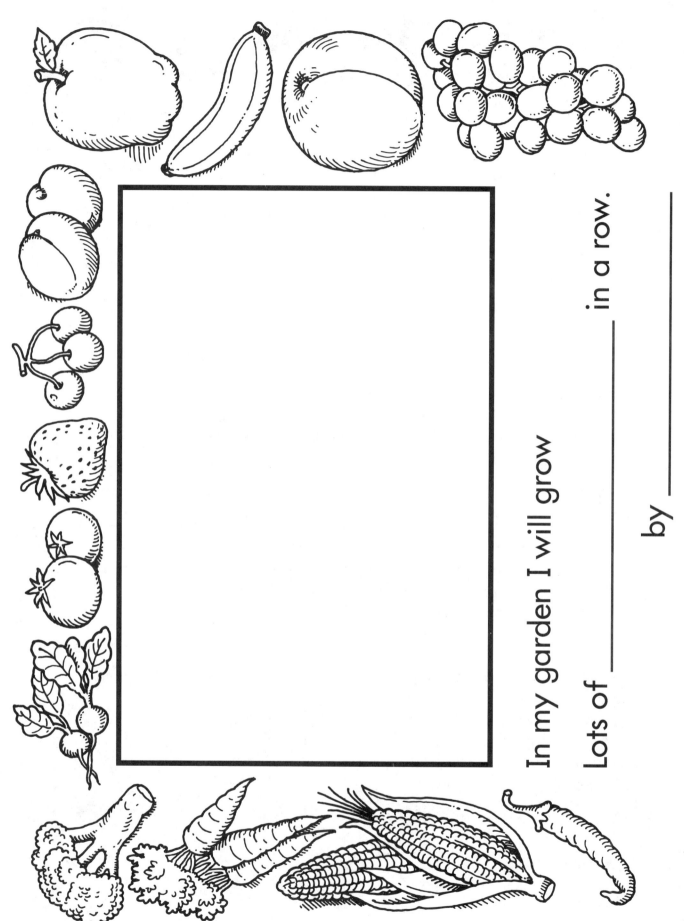

In my garden I will grow

Lots of _____ by _____ in a row.

Veggie Cards

tomatoes

corn

green peppers

pumpkins

cucumbers

lettuce
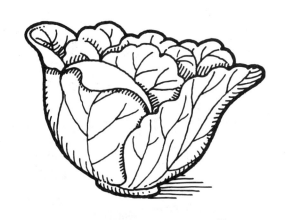

Veggie Cards

potatoes	onions
peas	green beans
zucchini	carrots

Counting Critters

Children will choose a zoo animal and a number to complete their page.

Materials

- *Counting Critters* reproducible (page 80)
- *Numbers* teaching aid (page 94)
- *Zoo Animal Cards* (pages 81–82)
- dice
- crayons or markers
- scissors
- glue

Class Book Directions

1 Copy a class set of the *Counting Critters* reproducible and *Numbers* teaching aid. Copy and cut apart several *Zoo Animal Cards* so children have a variety to choose from. Make additional copies of the *Zoo Animal Cards*.

2 Invite children to write a number or letter on the board for classmates to identify it as a number or a letter.

3 Have each child roll a die to determine which number page he or she will make. If a number has already been taken, a child will need to roll the die again. After the numbers 1–6 have been rolled, add a second die to roll the numbers 7–12 or roll the numbers 1–6 again to make two separate books.

4 Ask each child to choose a zoo animal card. Give each child a copy of the book page reproducible. Show children where they will write their number using the *Numbers* teaching aid, and where to write the name of their zoo animal—with a plural *s* if their number is more than one.

5 Call children up to count out the correct number of their zoo animal from the zoo animal cards. Have children take the cards back to their desk, color the animals, and cut them out on the dotted line. Invite children to glue the cutouts to their book page. Encourage them to draw a picture of their animal's habitat to complete the page.

Parrots are red,
We saw a few.

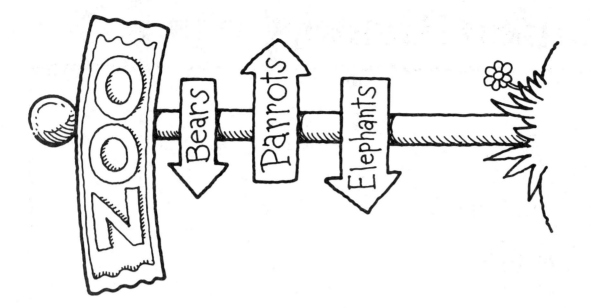

And I saw _____

by _____ at the zoo.

Zoo Animal Cards

elephant

zebra

giraffe

hippo

rhino

polar bear

Zoo Animal Cards

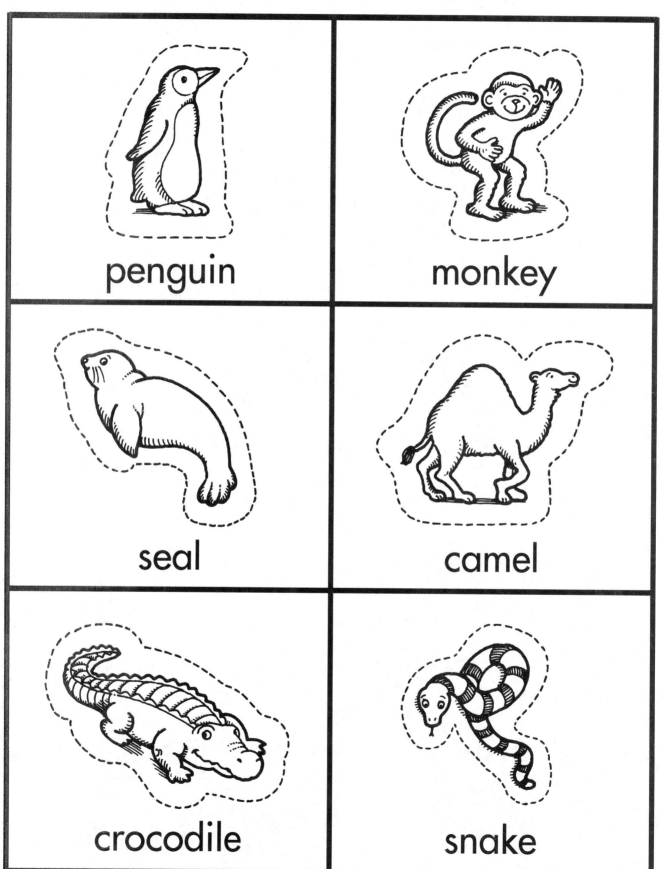

penguin

monkey

seal

camel

crocodile

snake

Farm Animals

Children will write a color word and a farm animal name, and they will illustrate a picture to complete their page.

Materials

- *Farm Animal* reproducible (page 84)
- *Colors* teaching aid (page 93)
- *Farm Animal Cards* (pages 85–86)
- crayons or markers
- index cards
- two paper bags

Class Book Directions

1 In advance, copy class sets of the *Farm Animal* reproducible and *Colors* teaching aid. Correctly color each copy of the *Colors* teaching aid. Copy and cut apart enough *Farm Animal Cards* so that each child can have a variety to choose from. Write each color from the teaching aid on a separate index card. Place the color words in a paper bag labeled *Adjectives*. Place one set of the *Farm Animal Cards* in a paper bag labeled *Nouns*.

2 Show children the two paper bags. Tell children that colors are adjectives because they describe something. Point out that the animal words are nouns because they name an animal.

3 Teach children the rhyme from the book page. Have the class say *I went to the farm and what did I see? I saw a . . . .* Have a child pull out an adjective and a noun from each paper bag and read those words along with the rest of the rhyme. Continue activity until each child has two cards.

4 Give each child a copy of the book page and the *Colors* teaching aid. Show children that they will be writing the color word on the line above the crayon. Next, show the class how to write the name of the animal on the second line.

5 After children have completed their writing, invite them to draw a picture of the appropriately colored farm animal.

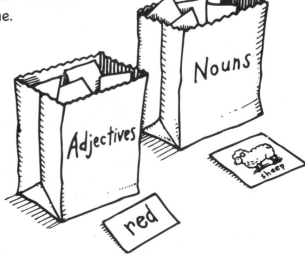

I went to the farm,

And what did I see?

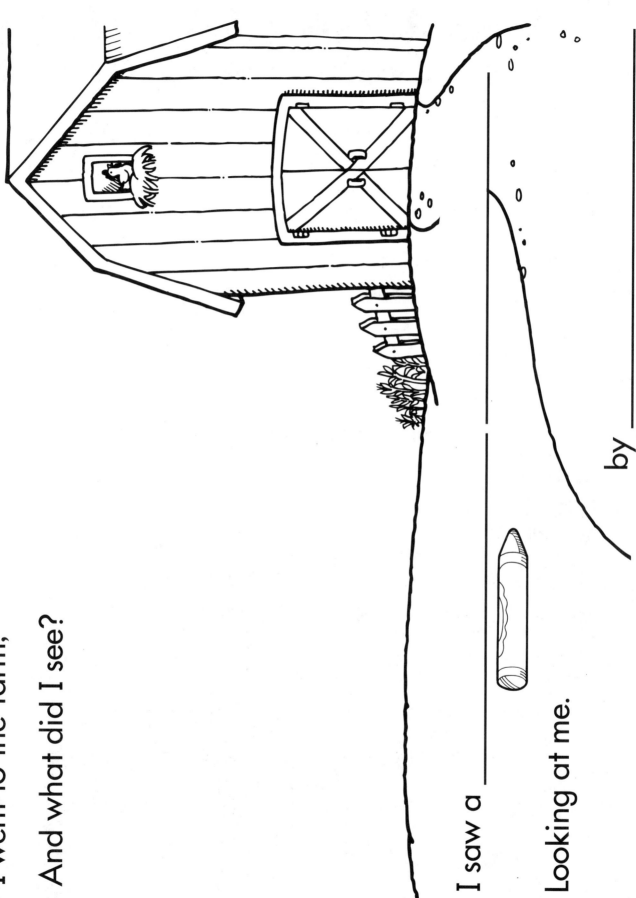

I saw a _____

Looking at me.

by _____

Farm Animal Cards

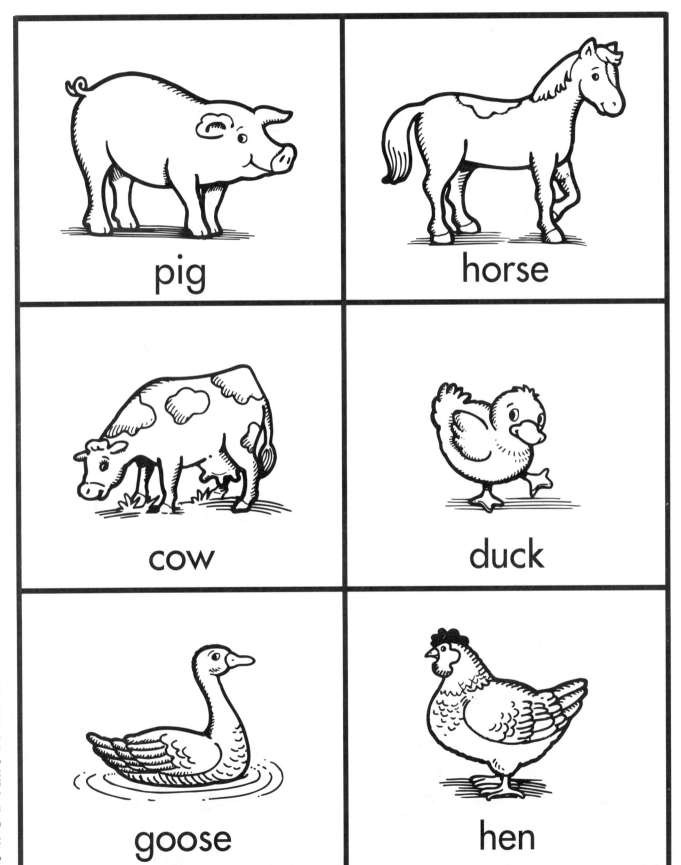

pig

horse

cow

duck

goose

hen

Farm Animal Cards

chick

sheep

goat

dog

cat

rooster

Marvelous Mommies

Children will write what their mom is an expert at and illustrate it to complete their book page.

Materials

- *Marvelous Mommies* reproducible (page 88)
- assorted colors of paint
- paintbrushes
- inexpensive frames (optional)

Teaching the Standards

- Dictate stories, poems, and personal narratives
- Use verbs in written compositions

Class Book Directions

1 Copy a class set of the *Marvelous Mommies* reproducible.

2 Talk with children about what an expert is. Explain that an expert is really good at what he or she does. Use children as examples (e.g., Jake is an expert at listening when the teacher speaks. Sara is an expert at writing her name.). Discuss how you could determine if people were experts in sports, computers, art, or music.

3 Tell children that mommies are experts at many things. Have children identify something their mommy is an expert at (e.g., rock climbing, fixing broken toys) and how they know this. (If needed, children can choose a grandma or other female family member or friend.)

4 Give each child a copy of the *Marvelous Mommies* reproducible. Have the children write or dictate what their mommy is an expert at on the first line and what they have seen her do to show her expertise.

5 After they have completed their writing, set out paint and invite children to paint a picture of their moms.

6 As an option, have children make two copies of their page. Purchase inexpensive frames, and place each child's page inside a frame to send home for Mother's Day.

My mom is an expert writer.

I've got to hand it to my mom!

She's an expert _____

because _____ .

by _____

Standards-Based Class Books © 2007 Creative Teaching Press

Farewell Friends

As an end-of-the-year activity, children will write a farewell letter to a child in their class.

Materials

- *Farewell Friends* reproducible (page 90)
- index cards
- hat or other container
- sentence strips
- pocket chart
- crayons or markers

Class Book Directions

1 Copy a class set of the *Farewell Friends* reproducible. In advance, write each child's name on a separate index card. Place the cards in a hat or other container. Also write examples of the different parts of a letter (i.e., date, greeting, body, closing, and signature) on separate sentence strips. Place these strips out of order in a pocket chart.

2 Tell children that they are going to create an end-of-the-year book. Explain that children will pick a name from the hat and write a letter to that child telling something nice about him or her.

3 Display the pocket chart containing examples of the different parts of a letter. Read it out of order to emphasize the importance of the proper order. Challenge children to help put it back in order.

4 Give each child a copy of the book page. Read the words on the page and explain that it is written in the form of a letter. Show children that they will copy the child's name that they pick on the first line, write what they like most about the child on the middle line, and sign their name on the bottom line. Have children choose a name and complete the writing by filling in the blanks. If they are unable to write the words on their own, have them dictate the letter to an adult.

5 To finish their page, invite children to draw a picture of the child they are writing to in the middle of their page.

Dear _____,

What I like most about you is

Your friend,

_____

Standards-Based Class Books © 2007 Creative Teaching Press

Super Dads

Children will write why their dad (or other male role model) is super and illustrate a picture of him.

Materials

- *Super Dads* reproducible (page 92)
- pictures of superheroes

Class Book Directions

1 Copy a class set of the *Super Dads* reproducible.

2 Show children pictures of superheroes. Explain that superheroes have special abilities and powers that normal people don't have. Ask children if they think their dad (or other special male role model) has any special talents or abilities. Explain that all dads are special and you would like to know what makes their dad a superhero to them. Point out that the special powers can be anything they really like or admire about their dad. For instance, a child might say her dad is a superhero because he untangles her fishing line.

3 Give each child a copy of the book page. Have children write why their dad or other male role model is a superhero. If they are unable to write it, have them dictate it to an adult.

4 After children have finished their writing, ask them to complete their page by adding a picture of their superhero father figure.

My dad is a superhero because

_____

by _____

Colors

○ red
○ blue
○ yellow
○ green
○ orange
○ purple
○ black
○ brown
○ pink
○ gray
○ white

- -

Colors

○ red
○ blue
○ yellow
○ green
○ orange
○ purple
○ black
○ brown
○ pink
○ gray
○ white

Numbers

1	•	one
2	• •	two
3	• • •	three
4	• • • •	four
5	• • • • •	five
6	• • • • • •	six
7	• • • • • • •	seven
8	• • • • • • • •	eight
9	• • • • • • • • •	nine
10	• • • • • • • • • •	ten
11	• • • • • • • • • • •	eleven
12	• • • • • • • • • • • •	twelve

Standards-Based Class Books © 2007 Creative Teaching Press

Letters

Aa	Nn	Aa	Nn
Bb	Oo	Bb	Oo
Cc	Pp	Cc	Pp
Dd	Qq	Dd	Qq
Ee	Rr	Ee	Rr
Ff	Ss	Ff	Ss
Gg	Tt	Gg	Tt
Hh	Uu	Hh	Uu
Ii	Vv	Ii	Vv
Jj	Ww	Jj	Ww
Kk	Xx	Kk	Xx
Ll	Yy	Ll	Yy
Mm	Zz	Mm	Zz

Letters

Dear Family,

We are very excited to be publishing class books throughout the school year. The books we will create focus on beginning writing processes and skills, and they are tied to national language arts standards. Through writing and reading these books, your child will also develop reading skills and greater self-esteem.

From time to time, a blank book page may be sent home for completion. We will have already done activities to prepare children to complete this page at home. Please help your child edit his or her page for publication and return it the next school day.

The children's finished pages will be bound together into a class book and then enjoyed in class. Many of these books will be sent home to your family for you to enjoy together. Read these books aloud to your child and ask your child to read it back to you. Please return each book when you are finished reading it so that other families can enjoy the book, too. We hope these books will become some of your child's treasured favorites.

We also may need some help in the book making process with writing children's dictation, assembling books, reading aloud books, or making book covers. If you would like to help us out or if you have any questions, please contact me.

Thank you,

Standards-Based Class Books © 2007 Creative Teaching Press